FRENCH RED

Poems As They Are

by

Timothy P. Banse

MIDDLE COAST
PUBLISHING

Good Books Are Where We Find Our Dreams

French Red
Poems as they are
by Timothy P. Banse

ISBN: 978-0-934523-24-0

Publisher's Cataloging- in-Publication data

Banse, Timothy P.
: poems as they are / .
pages cm
ISBN 978-0-934523-24-0

1. Poetry. I. Title.
PS3563.E756 .F74 2018

811.6 –dc23

DEDICATION

This book is dedicated to my patron,
without whose generous support,
this book of poems could not have been written,
yet alone published.

CONTENTS

FRENCH RED

I who have always believed too much in words,
am no longer surprised at the beauty
and the shamelessness of women.

One night I burned up all of my matches
to watch her smile in her sleep,
to look at the face I loved as a child.

An hour before,
when we loved,
I trembled to touch her unrepeatable secrets.

She.
With no fear of dying,
how she must dread the winter.
Who is the father of her winter?

On the road to her place
I passed miles and miles of fences.

In her walled meadow,
an old animal in its youth,
captured one that in the wild
that would never had reached such an age.

She had reason enough,
the way she was,
to want to be rid of me.

But I am the last one,
the last noble generation pursued
by the writings of settled peoples,

Remembering her kiss,
longing for her unrepeatable secrets.

And then,
I forget about her for years.

Flit

Bluebirds flit across the flowered meadows.
Yellow beaks picking up green bits of bush for the nest.
Robins eggs blue to the sun, waiting for life to crackle forth.
A forest of trees humming a symphony in the wind.
Spring grass weaves and wends with the warm wind of April.
Footsteps paired in love trod to the sky blue lake.
Fish smash and throw water.
Bullfrogs croak.
Stones and sand cushion the lover's backs.
Red wine lightens their soul.
Touch.
Warm and gentle gives pleasure.
A kiss, wet and wonderful is golden.
Close.
So close that it's one.
The pines cry with joy.
The eagle soars.
Man, woman and nature,
will to be one.

COGITO - OTIGOC

Je pense.
Donc je suis.

I think.
Therefore,
I think I am.

You think.
But you think wrong.

Not like me.

So think again.
Let me tell ya buddy.

AUTOMNE

Les feuilles tombent.
The leaves fall.
Leaves falling like raindrops.
The orchard floor is littered,
with her fallen leaves.

Soon enough we will all parasol to the ground.
Soldiers dying like flies on the beaches of Normandy.
Our brilliant colors will fade,
Burnt yellow orange bleaches yellow,
turns brown,
then crumbles into dust.

Next spring, the cold,
cold orchard will warm with brilliant rays of sunshine.
And those with sun-warmed shoulders will witness
Robins eggs the color of the pale blue sky.
Warmth will turn the meadow green.
Lilacs will blossom like a purple fireworks display.
Tulips throbbing red and pink and white.
Honeybees buzz and flit from flower to flower.
The air will taste sweet and fragrant.

None will remember,
her cast-off lovers,
or her dead leaves.

None will remember Autumn.
Les feuilles tombent.

Friends

Be a friend,
she whispers.
Just be a friend.
For now.

A need for time apart.
Let's just be friends.

For now.
It's hard to be a friend,
when once you held her in your arms.

Friends,
miles and miles apart.
Hold her close,
and dream that you know
what's in her heart.

Two buddies.
Miles and miles apart.

May I Have Your Attention Please!

You've been going out at sunset,
Whistling that little tune,
Thumb out on the corner,
Giving me hitchhiking blues.

Says she will never leave me.
Friend Mary says she will.
That a girl only love the man who'll hurt her,
and let the good ones go.

Well it's true children hate me,
and fathers never know,
why their eldest daughters,
all want to be in my next picture show.

Lock up your sister,
keep a close eye on your wife,
for I'm the villain who'll wreck your life.

It don't matter whether it's Cleveland,
or blowgut Chicago.

I'll mistreat your wicked women,
and they'll cry to see me go.
Will you?

Road shoes on forever,
My shirt sleeves never go cold.
Ladies all keep a lover,
and they hate me just like you.

7

Ladies there, I'm told,
like to keep a man tightly wrapped in pleasure.

Mournings in Oaxaca

Warm beer sipped
to wash down sardines in tomato sauce.
Eaten with stubby, frozen fingers,
on the desert rose.

Oaxaca,
my sparkling gem,
sky tall at 5,000 feet.

Copper-jacketed lead mows
across the billowing fields of spring wheat,
harvesting the young crop.

Crimson seeps wet into the black earth.
Stone walls stand pock-marked,
protesting the din.

Federal soldiers go home
to sleep in their own beds with the warmth
still tingling in their fingers.

That Clammy Feel

Close to the edge,
suffering the nagging feel,
of all of it about to tumble down.

Gunfighter syndrome?

The gritty feel,
of emotions lodged in the throat.

Souls waiting for one more
punch in the stomach
to make it all pop out.

Stuck in my craw
the disbelief.

The Simple Pleasure
of Her Golden Frame

Lust.
Life and libido,
blend in the eye.

I trust the will,
shall bring the body to shame.

A Favorite Word of Mine is Me

Not just to hear,
but to play the music.
Softly.

So softly it carries your soul
to the top
high up to the frozen air,
cold, blue snow.

Again she calls you.
Back to the music,
the love that she is.
Wend your way back,
to the song you know you need.

Now young
Growing old.
Be young today.
For tomorrow you are old.
As old as me.

Conscription Ain't Healthy

Blithering,
Babbling,
liquored lips,
teeth rotten with whiskey smell.

The soldier's head twisted
by cave man of war
lodged in his head
crushed in her steely maw.

Thank you, just the same
for the kindness
the pink skin
for letting me gaze into your eyes.

Let X = X

Smile darling.
Smile darling,
And show lot of Lips and Teeth.
Smiling a circus.
staging the drama,
of your dreams.

So who
do you
want to be
friend Timothy?

Not what possessions
do you want?

But who
is the intrinsic self to be?

Sculpting
the gaps
in personhood.

Be strong in such accomplishments.

Sam Sheridan

Riding on my horse
three days to the west
following a setting sun.

Anguish in my breast.
Whistling tunes.
Knowing that's the way it is,
around her.

And so it comes again
to rest on that spot
worn flat on the mind.
That rough place
holds it so well,
so firmly in place.

Keeping the Peace

Macramé
Needlepoint
Lux liquid
Hardees'
Tide
Rump roast
Afghanistan
Mr. Pibb
Pabst Blue Ribbon
Nitrosamines
The Pres.
Aircraft carriers
Tobaccy
CNN and Fox
If it's all so very important.
So why don't we care?

Stage Drudgery

Has no one told you about her Gorfian madness?
Nerves worse than coffee.
Shooting quarters from anxious hands.
into those machines like pilot's training.

The scenes are now boring.

Leave by the back door
as a fresh understudy
awaits his curtain call.

Hazy, brown, bitter eyes
fool you
because you've seen everything.
You've been twice to Phoenix
and seen more
than she'll ever sing.

Lines memorized
delivered with godspeed.
Didn't you know this was only opera
and not the real thing.
Costumes up
Hail!
Onstage!
it's curtain call!
Time for your performance!

This is the part where you must fall.
Not to her mighty sword,
but torn to shreds by a tongue as sharp as a wind in a

squall.
But don't pretend it's only play acting.
You're being paid to be on call.

Cinema *Vérité*

The movie's over.
It's time to go home.
Your ride is patiently waiting in the cold
in a shiny, new car
with fresh-smelling upholstery.

And now it's time
for you to go.

No more waiting
or silly saying
things you don't really mean.

The duel fought hard and bloody
on the back lot
didn't mean anything.

No one won.
I didn't lose.
But it's time
you and I
dance together in different ballrooms.

Thirst Man

Flying blind
one time
a scat talk musician
tastes the first night's set
with blood on the needle
in a scum brown world
shooting cottons begins.

The place where all the walls are dirty.

Read about my friend
on the liner notes,
the scat talk musicians,
hoping to turn the flip side of fame.

One day he black-inked all the scars he had.
flying blind
the turn off fate
that tried not to fry
a scum brown,
perfect thirst man
flyin' blind.

Moon Shine

Flash!
Bang!

Microwave!
His little Susie melted on stage
right in front of him
and now Jim just makes
and drinks
corn liquor.

These days there's just Jim.
Susie was doing him a slow hand lover.

It worked.
It worked so good the blast left him helpless
and a world blast full at him.

Left just Jim.
Working in what used to be Detroit
the buildings all fallen down,

No one cleans up the blowing papers.
These days there's only Jim.

.

Pistol-Packing Momma

The ragged tawdriness.
of her latest clothes.
and the glory around her nighttime
the streetlights round her home.

Glasses clink full of whiskey.
Whispers come and go
about a girl raised in Missoura
town Saint Joe.
Jesse James own mother
shot a man in those streets.
Blood filled the sewers,
shocked the townspeople into grief.

Ever since that day it's like a spell cast
on this woman from Missoura,
and the town of St Joe.

Don't wrinkle her flowers,
nor mess her gaudy clothes,
when you look at her presents
and watch the picture show.
It's a grade B movie,
and the invitations come and go.

Be a man about it, young, Isaiah.
Go slow.

Sometimes there's no reason for what has to be.
Happenstance hath no rhyme,
nor reason,

or conscience,
for you or me.

Grab hold the rails and slide
down to the ground floor.

Edge past the wolves, Dwayne
there is no more.
Give up all this boozing,
crying in her beer.

She wants a man to chase.
But not to catch.
And you're just too goddam near.

Make a present of the carnation
that grows in far off fields.
Let her beg you buy the pistol
and blast her stamina.

The "R" Word

Thanks for something.
The need for downers
Drugs
Booze
and lots of healing sleep.

Where nite storms flash across the prairie,
lightning bolts sear the vision.
Dust clumps into thick, red, mud.
Clogging the mouth
gagging the breath.

Looking for the Bones of This Old Child

Love is fragile.
And you are like an ape in heat,
a bull in a grocery store.

Is that you?
Beckoning me back for more blood-letting.

Let the barber do it.
He tells true tales
of big trout,
grain-fattened deer in the pines
and sly Indian guides.

Your stories are full of punk rock,
cheap American perfume,
and your sister's perils.

Dirty little girl.
A literary agent has more dignity than you.

Considerata

Go placidly. . .
You do yours . . .
The serenity to accept . . .
You know how it goes. . .
Sometimes
I puke up such babblings.

Dirty Child

Wobbly platform spikes.
And a down home crowd
that seemed to know one another.
Almost as if she were their sister
gyrating up there on that pedestal.

Big, floppy, blonde hair,
plastic boobs,
and oh-so-carefully manicured crotch hairs,
nearly hidden from public view.

She was sensational!
With her ceramic smile, pendulous boobs,
and erect nipples exciting all of us.
Wow!
What a boring woman.
I am all ready one experience too old for all of this.

The Urge to Meddle

Everyone's girl but mine.
Simply pour her a dream.
Love on the rocks.
Or, so I seems.
But if you're so smart,
why are you still afraid
to drink
the wine of empty dreams?

Life Below Zero

Grasp caution.
Brrr.
It's cold.
Ten below.
Shake snow from your wooly mitts.
Huddle cold by the fire,
warm your frosty nose.
Stand tall in the arctic bite
Spit out smoking laughter.
Do like your mother.
Rest your eyes.
Ignore the ears.
Close the mind.
There is no pain.

Blue Eyes

Watching from the door ajar
Smiling with laughter,
Black Thunder gives birth to Blue Eyes.
Sprinkling snow with her first breath,
she chats slowly with the earth.

Don't come near.
Don't brush my cloak.
Careful not to shatter my delicate balance.
Don't disturb my delicate beauty
that the world is unaware of,
or doesn't understand well.

With eyes like clear ice,
forcing the will of life,
her stubborn patience fills the gaps in personhood.

Her confused intimacy beckons with blood-soiled hands.
Silence from a distanc,
the wind whispers,
like ice.
In the cold,
closeness is lost.

Ripcord

I been long dead.
Been in trouble
A long time
Crashed and burned
when wings went bad
earth rushed up fast
packed dirt up my ass

When a bird falls,
he falls alone
you should have seen the feathers fly.

Harmonica Joe

He wants women.
Of course.
We all do.
He wants to give.
His price comes easy.
Can you play his tune?
God bless 'em.
Stories about Job.
Well I read the bible.
It's soothing stuff.
Everything ya' ever need to know.
Visit those pages before the fall.
Bibles on their knees
Thumbing past pages
Time will tell.

Hunter S. Who?

Hey!
I need some speed.
And the sparkly shine of an opal ring.
Nothing's going down to-nite.
So do some weed.
Pink hearts and a fried mind do sing.
Whiskey to burn my throat,
 and make a madman a maniac.
So whisper a promise,
to shout for joy when morning comes.

Kandide Kane

Cast off bow and stern lines
all ahead full into the millennium.

My God.
I know so much,
or am I a fool,
like Kane the warrior one.
cursed to never kiss death.
Cursed to know so much
that he must shed the cloak to bleed.

God blessed blood.
That coppery taste cloyingly thick on the tongue.

Scars heal.
New battles.
Eternal competition.
Forever.
Remember it all.
I do.

Babbling Again

Can you tell once you start where the fog will settle.
On the tongue,
or on fumbling fingers.

Where the primitive mind comes to rest.
How many ounces of gray matter
die per drink.

When the primitive comes to rest.
How welcome.
How lonel,
are the primitive thoughts.
Does he bunk in the back room.

No Place Like Home

A book.
A baby.
A toy.
3 kids .
And you.

Does she ever bother to tell the truth of what's new
today.

Hearts Like Gypsies

Cursed with gypsy blood,
a butterfly wings the meadow to see
red blossoms unfurl a pretty cloak.

Out pops a little girl smile, fresh with warmth.

She draws me near with kindness a good.
The ring of her laughter makes me smile.

Sadly blessed with her cautious love,
snow smokes waist-high drifts across my path.

Wallowing,
my silence rages as thunder.

Man blest with a burning ember dying in the snow.

Whispers

When the wind whistles through your ears
do you hear whispered secrets?

Are you like the willow?
The black locust?
The pine tree?
The white birch?
The sugar maple?

Letting weeping branches,
hang heavy with sap?

Relationships   Take   Work

Never let romance,
get in the way of love.

Living . . .
in spite of love.

Never let romance,
get in the way of your past.

Freedom.
Great goopy gobs of
fatuation,
gum-up the tracks.

Kilts, plaids and tweeds.
Winter woman,
cold, quivering.
Lips in need.

Only the lonely
Need to love.

My Kind of Lady
in the Middle of the Night

Do you know why men want women?
No.
Not just for that.
But why, that.

More than basketball,
muscle cars,
big bucks and power.

The why of all the energy and sport.
Why men want those long-legged blondes to beg for it.

Like a Scalded Cat

Listen to the bleak surroundings,
calling in vain.
First shouts,
followed by pathetic whispers,
then silent murmurings, turned inward.

Nick, my friend.
What goes with you?

When that delicate touch wanders around?
In your travels,
why not let it blow away
into delicate whispers of pink smoke.

Like flowers in the field,
losing fragrant petals one by one.
She is worse than a scalded cat on the run.

Rosie You're All Right

One time I saw red.
Breathed in the fragrance.

There's a woman I know.
She's like a flower
A rose
Roses are thorny bastard.
I got to hand it to you, Rosie.

Filthy Blonde Girl

Just a few scant glimpses
are all you get.

Look at the eyes.
Gaze at the wondrous beauty of her.
Her complexion,
Her eyeliner.
Her rouge.
Her hair,
Her shapely body parts.

With all this comes a price.
Can you pay?
Can you afford the trouble of her?
Stand to bear the prattle of her pals?

Care Package From Home

Ever since that morning in Tucson,
with her hand slap, slap, slapping,
I've had trouble with it all.

With all the noise and music.
The muggy loneliness of being with her.
Once I knew what was really in store,
I've had trouble with it all.

Clumps of filthy earth,
gumming up my shoes,
tired of all the walking,
when I don't know where I'm walking to,

Clean snow gone dirty.
Tawdry goodness gone sour.
A kiss on the lips gone bitter.
The muggy loneliness of being with her
fearing it never works
for nobody.
Never.

What Wonderful Madness

The electro-shock fellows
I know
frizzy,
shaved heads,
trembling nerves
and sagging minds
razor cut wrists
all friends of mine.

Believe in guardian angels the big warrior kind.
Like Gabriel
his sword raised high
to do battle
with Lucifer's Legions
and I.

Lilacs and Love

Lilacs are purple, yet some are not.
And I love you more than anyone else.
But there's all the others I've forgot

Absence makes the heart grow fonder.
Unless you're gone too long.
Thanks a lot.

Love is a red, red rose,
under the petals are thorns.
Please stop.

Never try to possess her.
Don't draw the strings tight.
But she still wants wedding bells to ring.

Be hers
and hers yours.
Except for the occasional fling after you tied the knot.

Love her as a red, red rose.
Tiptoe the line.
Never feel the doors swing closed.

Motorhead

Racing wild,
like a piston engine,
about to throw its valves,
right through the top of its head.

Screaming.
Too much air and gas mix.
No governor to hold things tight.

Climbing high,
10,000 rpm strong,
the valve train will self-destruct.

Pistons cranking out great gobs of torque.
Pumping oil.
Exhaust blatting out with a great, big roar.
The end is near.

No Such Thing as Merwyn

It's true what they say,
About old W.S.
and his three tricks,
the Spark,
the Flame,
the Glowing Ember.

W.S.
and his women
lay dead.
On the road to their friend's house.
Past miles and miles of fences
Painted up with.French Red.

Tired of passion.
Wearing thin their shoes.
Like witches,
the three tricks burned up.
hidden away with the spoiled milk
and the other items gone sour.

What was he like living that way?

Signs Everywhere There are Signs

STOP
Look
Listen

Ignore what you learned above.
PROCEED!
Do
Feel
Will

Ignore what you learned above.
REFLECT
Love
Give
Hope

Deny what you feel.
Better not get hurt
Might feel pain
Might feel nothing at all.

No!
Don't!
I won't

So why should you.
Don't stop, look, listen,
or believe.

LIE
RUN
HIDE

Good Old Michael

Good old Michael, she says,
As his reward he is made human,
and falls in love with her himself.

She murmurs,
No, I'm not searching for rainbows,
and not searching for gold.
All I want is to have you near,
as I grow old.

So sure it's not easy.
So bring me a morning,
a morning with you.
With plenty of sunshine
and nothing to do.

Make it last into late morning,
loving you.
You're smiling and the sunshine will warm us awake.
Your warm touch.

Make it a morning, a morning with you.
With lots of flowers, a kiss or two.
Your smiling eyes can never miss.
We'll walk in the garden, skip stones on the water.
Dancing forever, just me and you.

Until the next sunny day,
I will tell you I love you,
then send you on your way.

A Few Words About the Poet

Timothy's *nouveau oeuvre d'arte*, this book, explores his favorite subject matter, the beauty that is woman. He wrote many of the poems in this collection while hiking in the French Pyrenees, walking twelve-miles a day on the 500 mile long Camino Frances pilgrimage, at night bundling up warm against the frigid cold at in refugios. Fingers frozen stiff, burning up all his matches to warm and thaw them, provided the inspiration for the title poem.

His favorite colours are divided between Rose Carmethene and Alizarean Crimson, and of course, French Red. His favorite food is *Pork Rinds Provençale* his favorite musical group is, or was, the Irish Folk Singers Tommy Makem and the Clancy Brothers. His favorite classical music is Johann Strauss II's most famous waltz, Tales from the Vienna Woods, which features a virtuoso part for the zither.

Once a world traveler, these days Timothy lives a sedentary, humble life in small town Iowa where he lovingly dotes over his many grandchildren.

His biography was listed in 1979 Edition of Maquis' Who's Who in the World. - the editors -

www.ingramcontent.com/pod-product-compliance
Lightning Source LLC
Chambersburg PA
CBHW060539030426
42337CB00021B/4337